HERBAL
ABORTION

a woman's d.i.y. guide

Contents

Introduction

Since before recorded history women have been able to control their own fertility using plants. Whether it be for increasing the chances of conceiving, contraception, abortion or starting delayed periods, women have known how to listen to their bodies and affect them. It's only fairly recently that we've given over all knowledge of our bodies to medical professionals. My aim is to empower women to take the personal experience of abortion from the hands of doctors and politicians.

Until medieval times, midwives were the ones with the information about abortive and contraceptive herbs, and because of it they were burned as witches by the Christian establishment. The clergy recognized the power of fertility control and took it for themselves. Politicians inherited and still wield this power.

There was never any contradiction between the role of the midwife in childbirth and her role in dispensing herbs for abortion, it was seen as two different aspects of the same thing; part of the same cycle. I believe that regulation of your fertility must include being able to decide when to become a mother and when not to.

Although obviously an emotional time. abortion can be a positive experience, providing your fertt1ity, clarifying relationships and exploring your feelings about motherhood. It's not necessarily the opposite of motherhood. it can be part of it.

Widespread information about how to use these herbs has never been properly recovered. I decided to make it my mission to distribute this information after finding myself pregnant and not being able to find accurate, reliable information about herbs in time. It's easy to find a list of herbs to 'avoid during pregnancy', but this is a long way from knowing how much of these herbs to use to end that pregnancy.

This pamphlet should be read in its entirety with attention being paid to risks and side effects. There are risks involved with herbal abortion but these risks are no reason not to attempt it provided you are armed with good information about all the possible outcomes and are willing to resort to visiting a doctor if you need to.

You may decide after reading this pamphlet that herbal abortion is not for you. It's true, it won't suit everyone. Herbal abortion can only take place in very early pregnancy and has a reasonably high chance of failure. You may not wish to go through two weeks of taking strong herbs only to have to have a clinical abortion after all (and it is vital that you do not continue with the pregnancy after you've take herbs for reasons stated later).

Many of these herbs are quite toxic and can be taxing on the body, it's not true to assume that herbs are a less physically stressful method than a clinical abortion. Natural does not automatically equal safe. However, some of you may believe any attempt to take matters into your own hands to be worth it even if unsuccessful.

You should also be aware that herbal abortion is not an easy option, it involves dedication and focus and would be best attempted if you have some time on your hands and supportive friends around you.

All of this information goes hand in hand with knowledge of your own fertility cycle. Through making simple observations it's possible to determine when you are at your most fertile, and therefore when you are likely to have

2

conceived. This is basic information about our own bodies that more women should know.

Most of the information contained here has been gathered from other sources, and several names crop up regularly. Full details of all the publications and websites I quote are in the Bibliography. The amazing website by Sister Zeus was my first introduction to the topic and is the place where most of my information comes from. I would advise anyone who's thinking of attempting a herbal abortion to visit the website and join the email support group.

Good Luck
   Annwen

When to use the herbs

Firstly, a note about dating the pregnancy. Pregnancy is usually talked about in terms of weeks. I'm using the start date as the date of conception as this will be the exact number of weeks for which you have been pregnant. This is very easy to determine if you know your own menstrual cycle and can tell when you ovulated, or you may know the date of when you had unprotected sex. If you can't determine the date of conception then you can use the rough estimate of two weeks before your period is due. The medical profession numbers a pregnancy from the beginning of your last period so remember that if you're reading any medical literature or have spoken to a doctor, their date will be roughly two weeks before you actually conceived.

As a general rule, the herbs are safer and more effective the earlier on in your pregnancy they are used. so time is of the essence. There are several windows of opportunity for ending a pregnancy during the first six weeks (from the date of conception).

The best time to begin is during the first two weeks. This is the time between conception and the expected time of menstruation. In the first few days of pregnancy the fertilised egg can be prevented from attaching itself to the wall of the womb, this is how the medical emergency contraceptive (the 'morning after pill') works. If the egg has already implanted then its 'grip' will be weak as the placenta will not have been established and so it is still a very good time to utilize the herbs, this is when the pregnancy is most fragile and easiest to disrupt in various ways.

4

Another reason why this is a tune when the herbs are at their most effective is that many of these abortive herbs are thought to be teratogens. Teratogens cause the development of abnormal structures in an embryo resulting in deformities in the foetus, and have been linked to complications during pregnancy and birth. Fertilised eggs are thought to abort if exposed to teratogenic agents during the first two weeks of pregnancy.

If herbs are successful at this early stage then menstruation is likely to occur at the usual time-bleeding won't start much sooner than expected because a woman's menstrual cycle must complete itself before bleeding begins.

The next stage, when menstruation is due or just late is still a good time to begin taking the herbs, and they are effective until two weeks after the usual menstruation time. The chances of success are thought to diminish after this time, although successes have been reported.

However, Susan Weed talks of a final window of opportunity for the herbs to be effective by beginning to take them during the 5th week of pregnancy. The reason she gives for this is that most natural miscarriages happen during the 6th week. of pregnancy (when menstruation is about a month late - when you would bleed if not pregnant). She describes the body as 'remembering' bleeding at this time. I can't explain this phenomenon in any scientific way, but I have read successful herbal abortion stories that describe the abortion happening at this time even though the herbs bad been given up on for at least a week before this, which would support the theory of the body's natural cycles still having an effect

The herbs can be continued up until the beginning of the 7th week but **must not** be taken beyond this time as any miscarriage during or after the 8th week (given that the herbs can take a week or more to work.) is dangerous. This is because the placenta is firmly embedded in the uterine wall by this stage, meaning that in the event of a miscarriage the umbilical cord is likely to break leaving the placenta inside the uterus when the foetus is expelled. This can cause profuse bleeding, haemorrhage or serious uterine infection which could be life threatening. The chances of the herbs working after the final window of opportunity is extremely low and so it is not worth the serious risk to your safety.

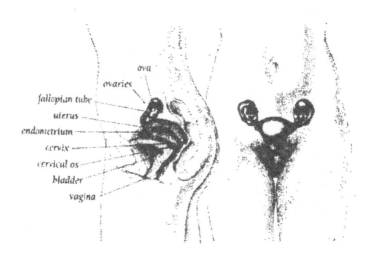

How to Use the Herbs

The herbs can be taken iis tea. tinctures or capsules. The idea is to keep a constant level of herbs circulating through your body, so for this reason you should take the herbs at regular intervals throughout the day and night. Set the alarm to wake yourself at least once or twice in the night to take a dose, as a whole night without herbs could undo any progress you've made during the day.

I would recommend taking time off whatever else you're doing in or r to focus on the task in hand, as it could prove difficult to take your herbs frequently and regularly if you're travelling or very busy. Herbal abortion is not easy and requires you to be focused. Your chances of success are increased, in my opinion, if you give yourself time.

Discontinue the herbs once bleeding has begun, if you only get a little spotting then continue until you have blood flowing properly. Herbs should be used for a maximum of 10-14 days. This is because the herbs and dosages we are dealing with can be very stressful on the body. The risk of doing serious damage to yourself is too great, don't put your own health and even life at risk (as damage to the vital organs can occur if you overdo the dosages or continue beyond the upper limit of two weeks). These herbs are strong and so your body will feel taxed but it's very important not to risk poisoning yourself. Stick to the recommended dosages.

Some herbs are more toxic than others and it does not follow that the most toxic are the most effective in causing abortion. As with all medicines, a herb can cause different reactions in different people. Herbs which could cause very bad side effects in one woman could be fine for another so listen to your body and choose the ones which are best for you. At any sign of poisoning discontinue the herbs that you are using.

Although this may sound a little patronising, you must ensure that you start using contraceptives immediately after the abortion. You may find that you ovulate at an unexpected time as your cycle will take a while to settle back into any kind of pattem (it could be earlier or later). May women have found themselves pregnant again at the next ovulation after the abortion so be careful!

Which Herbs to Take

Each herb has a unique action on the body and it is useful to know how each one works in order to select the right ones at the right time. The herbs have been categorised by their properties and some herbs appear in more than one category as they affect the body in more than one way. Many herbs could cause abortion single-handedly but a combination of complementary herbs could prove more effective. Choosing herbs with different actions to each other would be complementary, rather than using several with the same action. There is some evidence to suggest that using just one to four heJbs at a time is better than trying to combine a large number of herbs.

These categories could be seen as an oversimplification as wholeplants have a variety of different actions combining to make each one unique, but nevertheless these three basic groupings are an invaluable guideline for getting it right.

Progesterone Blocking Herbs

These are also referred to as 'implantation inhibiting herbs' as they are the category of herbs that are used as emergency contraception after fertilisation, but they're effective after that period as well. They work by interfering with the normal production of the hormone progesterone, without which the lining of the womb becomes unsupportive to the fertilised egg. Progesterone is crucial to the continued viability of a pregnancy. If the egg has not yet implanted in the womb then it is prevented from doing so and is expelled along with the lining. If the egg has already implanted, it detaches from the unsupportive womb lining and the lining will break down.

Cotton Root Bark

Wild Carrot Seed

Vitamin C

(not a herb, but included here because ifs readily available, effective and non-toxic)

Rue

(this is not a progesterone blocking herb, is placed in this category as it does cause the womb lining to break down. It does this by decreasing the permeability of blood capillaries in the womb)

Uterine Contracting Herbs

These herbs cause contractions in the uterus, which can expel the embryo and are an ideal addition after a progesterone blocking herb has been used for a few days. Often these herbs can help to regulate and strengthen any contractions that are **happening** due to the use of other abortifacients.

Angelica root

Dong Quai (Chinese angelica)

Blue Cohosh

Cotton Root bark

Pennyroyal

Juniper

Mugwort

Tansy

Some herbs cause uterine contractions because they are oxytocic. This means that they stimulate the pituitary hormone Oxytocin. This is a hormone that stimulates contractions during labour but is suppressed by the body's production of progesterone until the final stages of pregnancy. **Oxytocic herbs: Cotton Root Bark, Blue Cobosh.**

Some herbs cause contractions because they contain the volatile oil thujone.

Thujone also stimulates the brain and is toxic in large doses. Thujone is present in many herbs including, most famously, wormwood which is used to make the mind altering drink absinthe popular in 19th century France. If used in a concentrated form or in extremely large doses thujone can cause delirium, hallucinations, convulsions and brain cortex lesions. Thujone has been known to trigger epileptic seizures and so herbs containing thujone must be avoided by those with epilepsy. These herbs should be used with caution and without exceeding dosages stated. In my opinion, there are many other herbs that are far less toxic to use before selecting any from this category. **Thujone herbs: Juniper, Mugwort, Tansy.**

Oestrogenic Herbs

These herbs contain a number of chemicals that are similar enough to the female hormone oestrogen to mimic its effects on the body. Oestrogenic herbs are thought to be teratogens, which could explain their effectiveness as abortifacients, but as most of these herbs are also found in other categories then it is likely to be one of a number of properties working together. Oestrogenic herbs can cause oestrogen-like side effects e.g. abnormal blood clotting, liver problems, and oestrogen dependant tumours, but are far less strong than oestrogen itself as found in the contraceptive pill. Anyone taking the contraceptive pill, any other oestrogen medication or blood pressure medication should avoid these herbs, as should anyone who's been advised against taking oestrogenic medication (like the contraceptive pill).

Black Cohosh
Blue Cobosh
Wild Carrot seed

Pregnancy Testing

The most responsible thing to do before attempting a herbal abortion is to confirm with a test that you actually are pregnant. There are many reasons for this. Firstly, herbs for tenninating pregnancy arestrong and can be stressful for the body, therefore if they're not needed they should not be taken. Another reason is that if you take herbs and begin to bleed but only lightly or for only a day you will need to know if you were pregnant in order to know if this is a problem. If pregnancy has been confirmed this could suggest an incomplete abortion which would require medical attention (see the section entitled 'what could go wrong'). However, if you are not pregnant then there's nothing to worry about.

As we have readily available early detection pregnancy tests there is still time to employ the herbs after a test. Tests are available that can detect pregnancy at 8-12 days after conception.

I'm aware that this contradicts the message to use the herbs as early as possible in the pregnancy, and whilst it is safest and most effective to begin as soon as possible, this must be weighed up against the possible dangers to health of using herbs when pregnancy status is uncertain. Remember, using an early detection test only means a delay of a few days, which leaves you well within a safe time scale for disrupting pregnancy and to seek a clinical abortion if this should fail.

Home pregnancy tests work by measuring the presence of the hormone 'human chorionic gonadotropbin' (hCG) in your urine. This hormone is produced by the placenta shortly after the embryo has implanted in the womb lining and begins to build up rapidly, doubling almost every 48 hours up to the 60th-90th day of pregnancy.

Not all pregnancy tests are the same; some are more sensitive than others. Unfortunately pregnancy tests rarely print their sensitivity on the packaging - they usually say that they can be used from the first day of a missed period even though some can be used several days before. The following table has been compiled from information gained by contacting manufacturers. The table is by no means complete as yet; research is still ongoing into other brands. If you have a test that you are unsure about it's sensitivity it's often possible to gain the information by ringing a phone number on the packaging.

The most sensitive test I've discovered is Easistix P which is produced by Eastern Pharmaceuticals[1]. Unfortunately it isn't one of the most widely available, I found it in my local chemist but not in any of the supermarkets, it's also possible to order it over the internet[2]. Funnily enough, there is a pub in Derby that has a vending machine that stocks this brand of test in the Ladies toilets[3]. If you can't find Easistix P then any of the tests which can detect 25 mlU of hCG would be fine. The tests that detect 50 mlU of hCG are not classed as early detection tests and should be avoided unless menstruation is already late. Knowing the date you last ovulated is an extremely valuable piece of information in this situation so that you can determine exactly when conception occurred. If you have a regular 28-day cycle then you are most likely to ovulate on day 14 or 15 and so you can use the 25 mlU tests 3 or 4 days before your period is due.

---

[1]   Eastern Pharmaceuticals ltd, Comb House, 7 St Johns Road, Islewort, Middx TW7 6NA

[2]   www.westonshealth.co.uk/acatalog

[3]   The Woodlark Inn, Bridge Street, Derby

Name of Test	Sensitivity	How early you can use it (only a guide)
Easistix P	15 mIU	8-10 days after conception
First Response	25mIU	10-12 days after conception
Rapid self test	25 mIU	10-12 days after conception
Unichem	25mIU	10-12 days after conception
Early Bird	25mIU	10-12 days after conception
Reveal	25mIU	10-12 days after conception
Boots own brand	50 mIU .	The day your period is due
Predictor	50 mIU	The day your period is due
Clear Blue	50 mIU	The day your period is due

The lowest concentration of hCG detected by each test is measured in mili International Units (mIU). The lower this number, the more sensitive the test.

For more information on bow to determine when you were fertile and what your risk of pregnancy would therefore be see www.sisterzeus.com/risk_of_preg

If you have irregular periods: Irregular periods make it difficult to determine when you ovulated and therefore when to use a pregnancy test. Sister Zeus[4] advises using three pregnancy tests in this situation, the first twelve days after unprotected sex, the second two days later. If both tests are negative then the chances of pregnancy are low, however, a third test is advised, a week later, to make absolutely sure.

False Negative results

If you get a negative result from your test then there is still a chance you are still pregnant. This is because there is a possibility that the levels of hCG have not built up sufficiently in your system to be detected by the test, this is especially a risk at this early stage. If you get a negative result, but you still feel pregnant, test again 48 hours later (as levels double roughly every 48 hours). False positive results are very rare.

---

[4] www.geocities.com/sister_zeus or www.sisterzeus.com

14

The Importance of a Back Up Plan

It is vitally important that you've made a firm decision to terminate the pregnancy before you attempt herbal abortion. Herbs are not a totally reliable way to end a pregnancy (estimated at just under 50% effective, but I don't know how this figure is arrived at as no scientific research has been undertaken on the subject as far as I am aware). If you are not successful it is *essential* that you don't carry the pregnancy to term. The effect of these herbs on the developing embryo is largely unknown. Many of these herbs are believed to be teratogens, which are substances that cause the development of abnormalities in an embryo, which could result in a severely deformed foetus. This early stage of pregnancy is when all of the embryos bodily organs and systems are forming and so are highly vulnerable to damage. These herbs could also cause problems with the placenta (causing it to partially detach or develop abnormally) which could not only damage the embryo/foetus but also cause dangerous complications in labour.

It is therefore *absolutely crucial* that you are prepared to go through a clinical abortion before you attempt a herbal one.

Whilst technically abortion could be refused, it is in effect available on demand in the UK. The permission of two doctors is required to approve a termination, although often the second doctor is simply a rubber stamp. A doctor must approve an abortion if they believe that the mental or physical health of the woman would be at risk if she were forced to have the baby. Many doctors believe that simply having an unwanted baby would be enough to put the woman's mental health at risk. Other doctors might want to bear more information about why having a baby would be distressing to your mental health, so be prepared. Doctors who have a specific conscientious objection to abortion are obliged to refer you to a doctor that does not. Visit your family planning clinic or ring NHS Direct if you are unsure about the attitude of your doctor.

Abortion Is available on the NHS and most women report no problems in obtaining one. However, as in all areas of public health care, budgetary restrictions apply and not all abortions are publicly funded. In Scotland 96% of all abortions are NHS funded but in England and Wales the figure is usually lower. Eight English health authorities have admitted that they set specific criteria (over and above any outlined in law) to prioritise women for free abortion. It's not clear whether they fund abortions for women who do not come wider these categories. A full list of the health authorities and their categories is in Appendix I. Some of these categories include being on benefits, being under or over a certain age, being a student, already having several children, having had previous abortions. If your health authority has restrictive criteria and you do not meet them, you could consider lying (although they may require proof of income) or try moving to another authority temporarily (e.g. stay with a friend or relative). Some health authorities also fund abortion related counselling.

Your clinical options

Medical Abortion: If you are no more than 7 weeks pregnant (or nine weeks from your last period, which is how the medical profession date pregnancy) you can ask for the 'abortion pill' called RU 486. This involves taking a tablet to induce miscarriage and your body expels the embryo without the use of surgery. The experience will vary from woman to woman, but contractions are likely to be quicker and stronger than with a herbal abortion.

You will be normally be under medical supervision in a hospital for the few hours that it's likely to take, although some health authorities allow it to be taken at home. At home there's the comfort of familiar surroundings and control; in hospital there's the comfort of strong painkillers should you need them.

For more information on the development and history of RU 486 see *'Woman's Book of Choices'* by Rebecca Chalker (in the bibliography).

Surgical Abortion: This involves having the embryo removed surgically by a doctor. This is usually done under general an aesthetic, but can be under a local anesthetic. You don't usually need to be in hospital for more than a day.

Useful contacts:

Family Planning Association
Charity offering free help and advice if you don't want to go to your GP. They offer a very complete service including contraception, morning after pill, pregnancy testing, abortion referral, and information about councelling . Beyond abortion, their progressive work includes campaigns to improve sexual health and reproductive rights for all people in the UK.
www.fpa.org.uk
Helpline: 0845 310 1334 (9am - 7pm Monday - Friday)

British Pregnancy Advisory Service
Free pregnancy testing and campaign for abortion rights. Whilst they are a private organisation, they stridently and actively campaign for greater NHS abortion provision. If you are refered from a GP (or family planning clinic) you may be able to access their services for free.
www.bpas.org
Helpline: 08457 30 40 30

Brook Advisory Service
Free confidential help and advice on all sexual health and pregnancy issues

for under 25s.

www.brook.org.uk

Helpline: 0800 0185 023

NHS Direct

24 hours a day 7 days a week phone line offering confidential medical advice and information, including facilities available in your area. Staffed by qualified nurses and health visitors. Calls charged at local rate.

0845 4647

Abortion Law Reform Association

Campaigns to enshrine in UK law and in practice a woman's right to safe, free and legal abortion based upon her own informed choice.

www.alra.org.uk

There are other private abortion providers who do free pregnancy testing (Marie Slopes, etc). •

Be aware that some anti-abortion groups operate under the guise of free pregnancy testing and advice. If the logo includes a foetus or it's an offer of free post-abortion counselling from someone other than the NHS or local council, approach with caution. The most prevalent are Life (01926 311511 www.lifeuk.org and www.preghelp.org.uk). Another anti-abortion group is CARE (0800 028 2228 **www.pregnancy.org.uk),** who operate clinics under the name Alternatives Pregnancy Counselling Centre. I've given their phone numbers and websites as sometimes they're given out without it being clear who the organisation is.

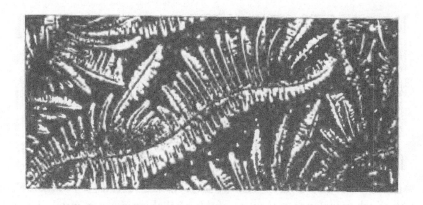

What to expect physically

The physical experience of a successful herbal abortion very much depends on how long you were pregnant. If the herbs were used before the second week of pregnancy the bleeding is likely to be a bit heavier than a normal period with slightly more cramps than usual.

As the pregnancy advances the abortion is likely to be more intense with more painful cramping and heavier bleeding for longer. If the pregnancy has advanced enough,you will see yellowish tissue with branch-like structures (chorionic villi), this tissue is usually enclosed in a blood filled sac. This is the beginning of the placenta and somewhere inside is the developing egg, which during the first 5 weeks will be as little as 1-5mm.

As soon as bleeding begins herbs should be discontinued to allow the body to do its thing. Expect a lot of blood but watch out for haemorrhage.

You mustn't use tampons, as the cervix is still likely to be relaxed and open thus making the uterus prone to infection. It's for the same reason that you should avoid vaginal sex until you stop bleeding. Using menstrual pads or a cup allows you to monitor the bleeding and examine what comes out. After the sac has been passed bleeding will slow down and gradually stop. Bleeding should last for around ten days. If bleeding lasts more than two weeks then it may be a sign of incomplete abortion and should be checked out by a doctor. Bleeding only a small amount, starting and stopping or spotting could also be signs of incomplete abortion.

How long will It take to work?

This depends on many factors e.g. your overall health, the strength of your reproductive system, the quality of the herbs. The herbal abortion could take as little as five days but usually longer. Do not take the herbs for longer than fourteen days (as explained earlier).

Herbs are not a totally reliable method of abortion and you may not be successful.

Spotting

If spots of blood begin to appear but blood is not yet flowing properly then you're close but not there yet. You may want to consider increasing dosages slightly at this point if you feel you're developing a tolerance. Or you could add another herb e.g. Dong Quai to increase contractions, or parsley or Black Cohosh to soften and open up the cervix.

If you're not sure if what's happening to you is normal, or if you want to confirm that your abortion was successful then you can go to the doctor and say that you've miscarried. You don't have to mention the herbs if you don't want to, as they'll treat you for miscarriage complications the same either way. Bear in mind that you may be referred to hospital straight away. •

If you experience any of the following symptoms you should seek medical attention right away:

1. Haemorrhage - Profuse bleeding. A large amount of blood is to be expected but if you soak a menstrual pad in an hour or less this is considered haemorrhage and must be treated immediately.
2. Fever - If your temperature is higher than 100.5° F / 38° C you could have a uterine infection caused by incomplete abortion.
3. Ectopic Pregnancy - If you experience a sharp pain in the abdomen.

particularly on one side, at any point during pregnancy you may have an ectopic pregnancy which is very rare but extremely serious.

Symptoms of pregnancy should begin to disappear very soon after the abortion (although it'll take at least 5-7 days for a pregnancy test to read negative). Remember that the herbs and indeed the whole process is hard on the body and you will have lost a lot of blood. You should rest and eat healthy, good food rich in minerals and vitamins, especially iron. Once the abortion is well underway and bleeding has slowed it would be a good idea to drink nourishing herbal teas to rebalance and rebuild your body:

- Using Echinacea for about a week following abortion would be useful for strengthening the immune system and warding off infection.
- Astragalus is a Chinese herb for rebuilding the immune system that can be used over a longer time period (three weeks on, one off).
- Nettle is a very valuable herb and can be helpful at this time to prevent haemorrhage due to its high Iron and vitamin K content. It can help rebuild the kidneys, which are often stressed during herbal abortion. It can also help relieve general stress, muscle spasms and cramping and has an overall high level of vitamins and minerals.
- Raspberry Leaf is a uterine tonic which can also be useful in preventing haemorrhage.
- Siberian Ginseng and St Johns Wort is a good combination for any low energy, mild depression symptoms.

Potential Risks

If you have any medical condition consult with a herbalist before using any of these herbs. This is particularly Important if you have high blood pressure, epilepsy, diabetes, liver heart or kidney problems, an IUD, or if you are prone to allergies.

Also if you've had a recent pelvic inflammatory disease or if you're taking any other drugs as the herbs may dangerously alter the way the drugs would normally work, or aggravate the medical condition being treated with the drugs.

Things that could go wrong

The most common problem with herbal abortion is that it fails to work. There is no certainty that the herbs will work on everyone, no matter how favourable the conditions are. If they don't work for you, the pregnancy should not be continued, as there is a serious risk of birth defects and complications during pregnancy.

There are several other risks you should be aware of before deciding to do a herbal abortion. Whilst these results are all possible, they are uncommon. Successful abortion is a far more likely outcome than any of the medical complications listed below.

- *Self-poisoning.* This can be serious as damage to important organs like the liver or even death can result from overdosing on some of these herbs. Do

23

not exceed dosages listed here unless directed by a herbalist. Reduce dosages at any signs of toxicity. Do not ingest essential oils as they can be fatally poisonous, as in the case of pennyroyal, essential oils must only be used externally. Remember not to take herbs for more than two weeks.

- *Haemorrhage.* This can be very serious, and unless treated it could be possible to bleed to death. Soaking a menstrual pad in one hour or less is considered haemorrhage so seek medical attention.
- *Incomplete abortion.* This happens when some foetal tissue is retained inside the uterus, and it can cause several serious problems:

1. The tissue can putrefy causing uterine infection which,if untreated, can result in sterility or even death. The first sign of infection will be fever followed by abdominal pain.
2. The uterus is unable to return to its normal size causing haemorrhage to occur. This may manifest as mild bleeding which lasts for an abnormally long time or very heavy or profuse bleeding.

Both of these situations need immediate medical attention. Most often a clinical abortion will be performed to remove the remaining tissue. In the case of haemorrhage a blood transfusion may **be** required. In the case of infection, antibiotics will be issued.

- *The herbs kill the embryo but do not expel it.* Bleeding begins but no tissue is expelled. Bleeding may only be slight or may only last for a few hours or a couple of days. Symptoms of pregnancy will persist, and a pregnancy test is still going to read positive even after a week. If you still have time you can persist with the herbs (remember not to exceed the 14 day maximum time). A sonogram from the doctor or clinic will confirm if the embryo is still alive, but either way, you will need to seek a clinical abortion.
- *Ectopic Pregnancy.* This is a rare condition, but is a risk to be considered with any pregnancy, not just with herbal abortion. It is when the egg becomes stuck in the fallopian tube and begins to grow there instead of in the uterus. This is a life-threatening situation as the growing egg may

rupture the fallopian tube. If you experience sharp pain in the abdomen on one-side you must seek immediate medical attention.

nettle leaves and flowers
urtica dioica

Other things that could assist

Many of the stories of successful herbal abortions that I have read talk of things you can to assist your progress, and so I've collected these tips together. This list is simply a list of things that I've heard and feel should be included but are circumstantial, and so are not as reliable as the rest on the information in this pamphlet. I realise that some of these things are what you least feel like doing in the early stages of pregnancy while you're feeling nauseous and tired. However, you are aiming to stop the body in it's tracks and so doing things that work against the natural impulse to protect your pregnancy is what is required of you. Almost all of the success stories I've heard have mentioned using at least one of these tips.

- *Orgasms*- whether from sex or masturbation, orgasms cause uterine contractions and many women swear that they were the key to ensuring a successful abortion. It could also be the relaxation of, and the improved circulation to the pelvic area associated with sex or masturbation that is also helping. There is also evidence to suggest that Oxytocin (the hormone which causes uterine contractions) is released during orgasm. This tip has been repeated by such a large number of sources that I have to believe there's truth in it.
- *Nipple stimulation* - This is more evidence to suggest that having lots of sex is a good thing to do at this time - you can of course do it during masturbation as well. The reason behind this one seems to be the fact that oxytocin is released when the nipple sare stimulated as it is a hormone which also has a role in milk production.

- **Exercise** - Many sources talk. of the role of vigorous exercise. Improving circulation will undoubtedly assist the herbs in their work, whilst the motion and movement might be helping to dislodge the embryo (I have heard nurses advising a woman to run up and down the stairs to hasten the onset of her medical abortion (abortion pill)). Women have talked of how exercise sends a message to the body that this is not a good time to be pregnant. Generally being as physically active as possible would assist sending this message.

- **Semen** - some women believe that the presence of semen in the vagina to be a factor in their success. This could be due to the fact that semen contains a chemical to soften and open the cervix to help the semen enter. However, I've also been told that this chemical is only present in such small amounts that it's not really useful for the purposes of abortion. Either way, I don't see how it could hinder! Frequent sex could also be beneficial for many reasons including those stated above. Maybe the general motion and stimulation of the cervix during penetrative sex is somehow useful in assisting the dislodging of the embryo.

- **Hot Baths** - this could be helpful by opening the blood vessels and promoting circulation, but water so hot that it bums you is *not at all* necessary - women burning themselves in desperation is a common old wives tale, there's no benefit in doing it.

- **Meditation** - If you practice meditation then it would be a good thing to use now. Some women believe that mentally focusing on releasing the spirit of the embryo can help, also visualisation techniques involving concentrating on the womb lining breaking down and blood flowing. It is sometimes said that the power of a focused mind can be as powerful as any medicine. Even if you don't practice meditation, focusing on the reasons for not being pregnant could be crucial during this time as it is a difficult process that requires determination.

- **Massaging the lower abdomen** - Massage techniques that are used to bring on, and assist in childbirth would be useful.

- **Acupuncture and acupressure** - I've heard one story of how an acupuncture session intended to relieve painful periods was instrumental in a herbal abortion. The woman in question reported feeling contractions during the session and abortion was successfully underway very soon afterwards. I've also heard that acupressure points can be stimulated in such a way as to induce abortion, but unfortunately I have no direct reference for this.

• Sitting on the toilet or squatting, and pushing down with your stomach muscles

• *Long bumpy car rides* - This is suggested on the Sister Zeus website, and could be effective as part of the general idea that activity and motion send your body the message that now is not a good time to be pregnant. I've heard of one woman who's herbal abortion got underway after an extremely bumpy ride in a 4x4 across rough terrain.

parsley
petroselinum crispum

Rh negative blood types

Accompanying everyone's blood type is a positive or negative symbol called the Rh factor, which denotes the presence of an antigen in the red blood cells (if you are Rh+, you have the antigen, and if you are Rh- you do not).

The following explanation applies to women who have Rh- blood types. I'm not at all certain how likely a scenario it is but as it is taken seriously by the medical profession, I am drawing it to your attention.

Isoimmunisation is a process whereby when a woman who is Rh- has a foetus with Rh+ blood and a minute amount of foetal blood mixes with her own. The woman's immune system reacts to the presence of the antigen in the foetal blood, producing antibodies to attack foetal blood cells. There is a chance of this blood mixing happening during abortion or miscarriage. This has implications for any future pregnancies this woman has, because if the foetus is Rh+ again, her antibodies would attack its blood cells causing severe anaemia in the foetus.If you believe you may want to have children at some point, you should consider this possibility.

If you have Rh- blood type and you have a successful herbal abortion, it would be a good idea to visit the doctor within 72 hours of starting to bleed as they can give you an injection to stop you producing antibodies (it does this by fooling the body into thinking it's already produced them).

I have read that foetal blood only produces it's Rh antigen in the 11th week of pregnancy, thus at the early stage we are talking about there would be no risk of isoimmunisation. However, I have not confirmed this fact and so would be very unsure about discounting any risk..

the herbal section

Dosages

The dosages I've given here are as precise as I can find. However,there are many factors *to* be taken into consideration meaning that dosages can never be exact. You must be prepared to use your own judgement and intuition. Potencies of preparations can vary, some tinctures that you buy are stronger than others are, and a herbs potency depends on factors such as, quality, freshness and how it's been stored. Different plants of the same variety can also have varying amounts of any given chemical because of naturally occurring factors.It is for this reason that when beginning any herbal treatment you should start at the lowest in the range of the dosages given, increasing or decreasing if necessary depending on how you react, and whether you experience severe side effects. Individuals may react very differently to each other and personal consideration can also play a part e.g. body weight,tolerance, sensitivity.

Purchasing herbs

Herbs are best bought fresh, however, are much easier to find in their dried form. When buying dried herbs, try to ensure their overall freshness. Herbs should smell fresh (not musty or mouldy) and look fresh (flowers and leaves still having their colour). Store herbs in airtight containers away from direct sunlight.

First choice for buying herbs is an independent health food shop or herbalist in your town. Chain stores like Culpepper and Neal's Yard usually carry a good range too. You will be able to buy the exact quantity you want and be able to check the quality If you cannot find a supplier in your town you could use mail order or online suppliers. Make sure that they have fast delivery before you order, as herbs that take weeks to arrive are no good to you.

There are numerous mail order places in the UK that sell some of the relevant dried herbs and even more that sell fresh herbs. However, we've only listed ones we know do fast delivery and/or organic supplies.

Baldwins
Superb supplier of a comprehensive range of dried herbs, including Dong Quai, Black Cohosh, Blue Cohosh, Rue, Pennyroyal, Mugwort, Juniper, and Tansy.

Fast delivery, online ordering
www.baldwins.co.uk
sales@baldwins.co.uk
Shop: 171 Walworth Road, London
020 7703 5550 (9am-5:30pm. Mon-Sat)

The Organic Herb Trading Company
They carry a wide range of herbs including Dong Quai, Blue Cohosh, Pennyroyal, Tansy and Rue and can deliver in about 2-5 days. They work out reasonably cheap, but you have to buy in large quantities

www.organicherbtrading.com
01823 401205

Jekka's Herb Farm (fresh, organic)
www.jekkasherbfarm.com
farm@jekkasherbfarm.com
01454 418878

How to prepare herbs

Water based preparations:

Individual herbs have their own recipes but a basic guide for a standard decoction or infusion is 500ml of water to 30g of dried herb. Dosages given assume this ratio unless otherwise stated.

When using the fresh leaves or flowers you will need to use three measures as opposed to one of dried (e.g. three spoonfuls instead of one) to account for the extra water content in the herb. Woody stems and roots don't have a large water content and so the problem doesn't arise.

Infusion

This is the easiest way to prepare a herb and is appropriate when using leaves, flowers and non-woody stems of the herb. Infusions are also used when the substances you wish to obtain from the herb are readily soluble in water or boiling would destroy if the properties you need.

A simple infusion is made simply by boiling water and pouring it over the herb, and then covering it and leaving it to steep for 10-15 mins (or whatever specific time period is specified for that herb). This can be done in a teapot or in a large jar with a lid, then strained and drunk. You can make enough for several doses in one go but infusions deteriorate rapidly so need to be made fresh each day.

To make a stronger infusion use a strong airtight jar (Pyrex or thick glass is required). Pour the boiling water into the jar over the herb and leave for four hours at room temperature. The advantage of using a jar is that the tea can then be carried around with to make it easier to take your doses.

Decoction

This is used to ex.tract the active ingredients from woody, hard fibrous material (e.g. roots and barks). The herb and water are placed in a pan and simmered on a low heat (do not boil) for ten to fifteen minutes, or for a time period appropriate to that herb. A lid on the pan will ensure no volatile oils escape. Decoctions must be used before they begin to ferment which can be 1-2 days or even a few months if capped and placed in the fridge.

Syrup

Honey or sugar can be added to a decoction to increase the palatability of the brew and increase the shelf life for up to six months.A syrup requires equal amounts (by weight) of sugar to decoction (e.g. 250 ml decoction to 250g sugar).Honey is twice as sweet as sugar and needs half as much **(e.g.** 250ml decoction to 125g honey). Add the sweetener to the hot liquid. Increase the heat until the brew is almost boiling and then take it off the heat. Pour the hot syrup into a sterilized bottle and cap it. Once cooled the syrup should be stored in the fridge.

Alcohol based tincture

Alcohol is generally a better solvent for herbal properties than water and also acts as a preservative. Home made tinctures are probably not as useful in this situation as they take at least two weeks to make (some people think they should be left for six weeks or more), but you may wish to make tinctures to keep for emergency situations as, if stored well, they can last several years.

The advantages of tinctures are that they have a long shelf life, are easier to carry around, are more concentrated (so that you don't need to ingest as much fluid)and more potent.

You will need to use alcohol of at least 30% (e.g. vodka) in order to have a high enough water/alcohol ratio, 50% is ideal and will make a standard tincture (The dosages in this booklet assume a standard tincture is being). Higher percentages are much more effective for extracting volatile oils and alkaloids. Use 125g of dried herb or 250g of fresh herb. Pour 500ml alcohol onto the herb and close the container tightly (an airtight container should be used). If the herb and alcohol don't all fit in the jar then you can top it up the next day when some of the alcohol has been soaked up by the herb.

Using a 500ml jar and keeping it topped up is a good idea because spoilage is more likely if there is an air gap in the jar and any plant material is exposed to it. Keep the container in a warm place away from strong sunlight and shake well once a day for at least two weeks (although some say at least six weeks). Decant the bulk of the liquid and strain the residue through muslin (wringing out the last drop). Store the tincture in a dark, airtight bottle with a dated label on it.

Vitamin C

(ascorbic acid)

Information about the use of vitamin C as an abortifacient has been passed around the feminist community since the seventies. The Sister Zeus website has numerous personal stories of women who've used vitamin C successfully, sometimes in combination with herbs, to terminate their pregnancies.

Although vitamin C is not a herb, it's one of the less toxic and most easily found of anything available for terminating pregnancy. It also has a good rate of effectiveness when compared with herbs used for the same purpose.

Vitamin C can be used as an implantation inhibitor and as an abortifacient:

As an implantation inhibitor: Vitamin C stimulates oestrogen and inhibits progesterone which produces a very unfavourable climate within the uterus. The result of this is that the egg will not implant itself in the womb lining. (see 'vitamin C as an emergency contraceptive')

As an abortifacient: After implantation progesterone is still essential for the continuning viability of the pregnancy. This is because progesterone is needed in order for the lining of the uterus to continue being supportive of the fertilised egg and to prevent it from breaking down.

Vitamin C can and has produced abortion without the help of other herbs. Joy Gardener writes "Don't combine this remedy with other teas mentioned (she mentions Pennyroyal and Blue Cohosh) because they may counteract each other. Women who have used both remedies simultaneously have had less favorable results than those who used only one at a time. This may be because vitamin C is a powerful anti-toxin, so it could nullify the effects of the herbs." This is unconfirmed.

One combination that has been successfully used on several occasions is vitamin C with Dong Quai and Parsley. Vitamin C starves the uterus of progesterone, and then after 5 days Dong Quai is added to strengthen uterine contractions and expel the embryo. Parsley relaxes and softens the cervix.

The best type to use is Ascorbic acid, although Joy Gardner writes that calcium ascorbate or sodium ascorbate are also ok. Pure vitamin C is best, although any of the many vitamin C products would be acceptable. Choosing the product with the fewer additional ingredients would be best. so that you avoid taking large amounts of sugar, flavourings and other chemicals. It is suspected that bioflavinoids are added to vitamin C to protect against miscarriage. It is essential therefore to choose a product that contains no bioflavinoids. Rosehip is a bioflavinoid and should also be avoided.

Dosage

A range of dosages have been suggested from 6 grams per day to twelve grams per day. From reading the personal accounts of herbal abortion on the Sister Zeus website it seems that most success stories involve the higher doses. I would advise taking 10 - 12 grams per day.

You should divide your total grams for the day into equal doses equally spaced throughout the day, and as many times during the night as you can manage.

Safety

Anyone with sensitive kidneys or any kind of kidney problems should not use vitamin C. This is because excess amounts of vitamin C in the body are eliminated through the kidneys which can put them under strain.

People who take anti-coagulants (e.g. aspirin), who have sickle cell anaemia, or have difficulty metabolising vitamin C should consult a doctor before taking mega-doses of vitamin C.

Possible side effects

Most of the serious side effects involved with such high doses of vitamin C are only applicable if such doses are sustained over a long period. The 14 day usage we are talking about here mean that they are unlikely to occur.

Abdominal cramps, hot flushes, rashes, constipation, gas and diarrhoea, headache, fatigue, acid stomach and kidney irritation may occur.

www.mothernature.com have the following information about the safety of vitamin C: "Vitamin C is non toxic at levels far in excess of the RDA. Some individuals develop diarrhoea from taking approx. 2,000 to S,000 mg per day, while even higher levels do not bother others. High levels of vitamin C can deplete the body of the essential mineral copper, 80 take a copper-containing multi nutrient formula if you're mega dosing on C. High doses of vitamin C may also increase the risk of kidney stones in some people, although studies indicate that those who do not have a history of kidney stones, severe kidney disease or gout are not at risk. Because vitamin C may increase iron absorption, check with a doctor if you suffer from iron overload and want to take high doses of vitamin C."

Joy Gardner expresses concerns that high doses of vitamin C makes the kidneys used to excreting large quantities of vitamin C resulting in a deficiency when high doses are stopped. She suggests gradually decreasing doses over the course of three days.

Vitamin C as an Emergency Contraceptive

Two 00mg tablets (non-chewable) should be placed inside the vagina immediately following unprotected sex or condom rupture and repeated twice a day for three days. This increases the acid levels in the vagina which should kill off the sperm. There is no guarantee that this will be 100% effective but it would greatly decrease the chances of sperm making it to the egg. This may cause iirriation; soothe with Aloe Vera.

Vitamin C can also be taken internally as an emergency contraceptive during the time between conception and when menstruation is expected. Sister Zeus does not believe it is as effective as the morning-after pill, but it can be used if you are too late to use it (longer than 72 hours since conception). Follow the same procedure as using vitamin C as an abortifacient as above. The menstrual cycle has to complete itself, so bleeding will not begin much earlier than usual as a result of taking vitamin C.

Dong Quai or Chinese Angelica

(Angelica Sinesis)

Chinese, American and European angelica are three different plants of the same variety. The Chinese variety, dong quai, is the most scientifically researched of the group and reproted to be the best for use in herbal abortion. American and European·varieties, while not as well researched, both have reputations for having similar effects and have been used by herbalists for generations. Angelica root decoction syrup is reportedly used by some midwives to bring out the placenta after labour. Dong Quai's name can be written 'dong' or 'dang', and 'quai', 'quoi' or 'gui'.

The root is often referred to as 'female ginseng' and is described as having an affinity with the female constitution. Dong Quai has two very different effects on the uterus; it has the ability to *stimulate* contractions, and also to relax the uterus and thereby *inhibit* contractions. **The effect depends on how you prepare the herb.**

Dong Quai's <u>relaxing</u> effect on the uterus comes from volatile oils contained in the root. Volatile means the oils are easily destroyed. When the aim is to capture them, brew an infusion. The relaxing effect of Dong Quai is useful for dysmenorrhoea (painful menstruation).

When the aim is to <u>stimulate</u> strong regular co-ordinated, regualr contractions in order to bring on delayed menstruation or cause miscarriage/abort

41

ion, then a decoction is used. The simmering of the herb destroys the oils, thus leaving just the uterine stimulating properties.

There is disagreement as to whether a tincture is useful or not. Sister Zeus says that a tincture *is* useful as the volatile oils are not extracted into it. Uni Tiamat states that alcohol-based preparations (such as tinctures) only produce the uterine relaxing effect. I haven't been able to resolve this contradiction, so I'd advise sticking to a decoction or a syrup of a decoction.

Dosage

The root is the part used. Look for quality products containing only the root. Do not use the fresh herb. only use it dried. Toxins present in the fresh root are eliminated by the drying process.

Decoction: Simmer the chopped dried root in a covered pan for 15-30 minutes. Drink a 250ml cup every three to four hours.

Tincture: 5-15 drops in a cup of warm water every four hours (although some sources say not to use it this way).

Capsules: From reports on the Sister Zeus website, an effective dose seems to be 1,000mg every four hours.

Safety

People with a history of cancer or who are at risk of heart attack shouldn't use this hero. If you take blood thinning agents like aspirin do not use dong quai or other angelica as these have a tendency to increase bleeding.

Possible side effects

The one that's most concerning is the tendency to increase bleeding. This raises concern when this herb is used to end pregnancy as it can increase the risk for haemorrhage. If you decide to use this herb, pay particular attention to how much you are bleeding. To decrease the risk of haemorrhage, discontinue use of dong quai (or other angelica) once bleeding is established.

Angelicas are phototoxic, this means if you are exposed to strong sunlight after using the herb you may develop a rash. Insomnia may also be a side effect. If you experience laboured breathing or weak and rapid pulse reduce the dosage. Other possible side effects are dilated pupils and stomach pain.

angelica
angelica archangelica

Blue Cohosh

(Caulophyllum thalictroides)

Blue cohosh is a powerful herb from North America which has a wide variety of uses. Native American Chippewa wise-women used a strong decoction for contraceptive purposes. It is famed for its ability to trigger and hasten childbirth and deliver the placenta.

Blue cohosh is often used alone or in combination with other herbs for the regulation of the menstrual cycle and to ease painful menstrual cramps. It is also used in formulas to treat endometriosis chlamydia and cervical dysplasia. As a uterine tonic, it nourishes and revitalises the uterine tissue in a variety of circumstances, including after pregnancy, miscarriage, abortion or coming off the Pill.

Blue cohosh contains at least two substances that cause the uterus to contract; oxytocin (a hormone produced during childbirth) and caulosaponin, a unique substance found only in blue cohosh.

It is also an oestrogenic herb, meaning it contains oestrogen-like substances and can have oestrogen-like side effects (those with oestrogen-dependant tumours should not use this herb). If you are not supposed to use the Pill then you should not use this herb unless under the guidance of your herbalist.

It is commonly used with pennyroyal (an abortifacieot) and/or black cohosh which helps soften the cervix and relax the os (the muscular opening of the cervix). It also encourages co-ordinated uterine contractions and according to some sources black cohosh is used to temper the intensity of blue cohosh's contractibility.

Susan Weed has a high opinion of Blue cohosh when it comes to terminating pregnancy and spoke of using blue cobosb alone, although Sister Zeus thinks it's better in combination.

Dosage

The root is the part of the plant to use. Some sources state that the abortifacient qualities of this herb is best extracted in alcohol, avoid glycerine based-based tinctures.

Uni Tiamat gives these dosages:
   Decoction: Simmer for 20-30 minutes, 125ml-250ml three to four times a day.
   Tincture: ½ to 1½ teaspoons, three to four times a day.

Joy Gardener writes about pennyroyal and blue cohosh:

Put two tablespoons of blue cohosh, two tablespoons of pennyroyal and two tablespoons of peppermint (to improve the taste, may have some mild emmenagogue qualities) into a large jar. Boil 1½ litres of water and pour over the herbs, cap tightly, steep for 20 minutes. Add honey if desired. Drink in 5 to 6 doses throughout the day. She adds, 'menstruation should start by the sixth day. Bleeding should be not more than double your normal amount for the first day or two.' She notes that American pennyroyal is stronger than European.

Susan Weed gives these doses
   Blue cohosh should be taken as a tincture, 20 drops of tincture in a cup of

warm water every four hours.

OR, 20 drops each of blue cohosh tincture, black cohosh tincture and pennyroyal tincture (NOT the essential oil). Drink slowly in a cup of warm water every four hours.

OR 2 tablespoons of dried blue cohosh root, 2 tablespoons of dried tansy and 3 tablespoons of dried pennyroyal leaves. Put a litre of water in a pan with the blue cohosh and bring to the boil. Put the other herbs into a huge strong jar and pour on the just boiled blue cohosh mix. Tightly screw on the lid and leave for thirty minutes. Reheat to drink. If you want to use a tincture just miss out boiling the herb (but still boil the water) and add 20 drops of tincture to the cup of tea when reheated.

She advises a maximum of five days of these treatments.

Safety

Caulosaponin (present in blue cohosh) also has the action of narrowing the arteries to the heart so if you have a history of high or low blood pressure, heart disease or stroke then you shouldn't use this herb. Anyone with diabetes, glaucoma or kidney damage should consult a herbalist.

Blue cohosh is an oestrogenic herb and has oestrogen-like side effects, eg abnormal blood clotting, liver problems and oestrogen-dependant tumours. Do not use if you've been advised no to take the Pill.

Possible side effects

Pain in the limbs, vomiting, pounding headaches. Reduce doses if you experience these. Blue cohosh, like many of the abortifacient herbs, can be taxing on the kidneys. To redress this, Uni Tiamat recommends drinking nettle tea as part of your abortion aftercare.

Rue

(ruta graveolens)

Rue has been historically used as a tea to induce miscarriage by women all over the world from the Mediterranean and Europe to Latin America and North America. Rue contains two chemicals that we know have the ability to cause abortion during early pregnancy. One is philocarpine, which is used in veterinary medicine as an abortifacient for horses, the other is rutin (or vitamin P) which hardens bones and teeth and strengthens arteries and veins. Rutin decreases capillary permeability in the uterine tissues, which causes the womb lining to become non-nutritive to the fertilised egg. Rutin is sometimes available separately in capsule form.

Dosage

Infusion: 1-3 teaspoons per cup, 3 to 4 times daily. Boil the water first then pour boiled water over the dried hero. Do not boil the herb in water as this destroys the herb's properties. Steep for ten minutes.

Tincture: 5-15 drops, 3 to 4 times a day.

Capsules: 1-4, 3 to 4 times a day.

Safety

People who have heart,liver or kidney problems shouldn't use rue.

Possible side Effects

Rue is a very strong herb, stimulating the uterus and nervous system. Rue/Rutin should not be used in excess or on a prolonged basis as it can cause kidney irritation and liver degeneration. The essential oil is highly toxic and should never be used internally. When using rutin read the label. Using rutin capsules may make you feel anxious or fearful due to its effect of keeping adrenaline in the bloodstream. Reduce dosage if you experience severe stomach pain, vomiting or convulsions.

Rue
ruta graveolens

Pennyroyal

American pennyroyal (*hedeoma pulegoldes*)
European pennyroyal (*Mentha puleglum*)

During American colonial times a tablespoon of brewers yeast was frequently added to a freshly brewed cup of pennyroyal tea to induce abortion. This combination is mentioned in King's American Dispensatory in the late 1800s as 'reputed to be a safe and effective abortifacient'.

Pennyroyal is a well-known abortifacient which causes the uterine muscles to contract. It is said to be very effective and is sometimes combined with Blue Cohosh or mugwort.

European pennyroyal is also known as Creeping Pennyroyal, Pudding Grass or Cunningham Mint. with the taller version known as Upright Pennyroyal. Joy Gardener notes that American pennyroyal is stronger than European.

Dosage

The leaves and flower tops are the part used,and are effective as an infusion, or as **a** tincture added to hot water. No more than four cups (250ml each) a day, for no more than five days. Blue Cohosh can be mixed to help with cramping;three recipes including pennyroyal are listed er Blue Cohosh.

Infusion: Steep 15-30 minutes, 75ml-200ml every three to four hours.
Tincture: 20-60 drops (¼ to 1 teaspoon) every three to four hours.

If you have access to the fresh pennyroyal herb you can make an oil infusion by soaking the fresh herb in olive oil. This preparation is also for external use, it may be rubbed into the soles of the feet and into the abdomen. There are uterine points on the Achilles tendon - massaging them with pennyroyal-infused oil may also be helpful by encouraging uterine contractions. The oil infusion is not as concentrated as the essential oil. it will not irrate the skin and more liberal amounts may be used.

Safety

The essential oil of pennyroyal should **NEVER** be used internally even in small amounts: it is a deadly poison and it is not a pleasant way to die. The essential oil may be used externally only, but as it is extremely potent it can cause skin irritation. The tea poses little to no fatality hazard. Uni Tiamat writes, 'I have found pennyroyal leaf infusion to be very effective and safe in my own herbal abortion experience. Anyone with kidney disease or damage should not use pennyroyal'. Also, those with a history of kidney stones should avoid pennyroyal. She notes that if you have not had results by one week then discontinue, as extended use may damage the central nervous system, kidneys and liver.

All abortifacients can be taxing on the kidneys and liver. Anyone with health problems, especially with the liver and kidneys,should consult with a herbalist or midwife before using any of these herbs.

Possible side effects

Nausea, numbness in extremities, dimness, sweating. Too much is highly toxic and the essential oil is deadly. The most common side effect with this herb seems to be nausea, reportedly affecting the majority of women who use it.So if you choose to use pennyroyal then be aware of this, plan to take it easy and expect not to feel your best.

European pennyroyal
Mentha pulegium

Wild Carrot seeds

(Daucus carota)

Whilst the Latin name is the same for the wild as for the cultivated carrot, the plant is **a** different variety that commonly grows in hedges and verges allover the UK. The seeds will either have to be gathered from wild or bought from plant suppliers (but be very careful to specify *wild carrot seeds*) as they are not available from herbal stockists. Be aware that non-organic seed suppliers may have treated the seeds with chemicals to increase their germination rates.

The Wild Carrot is also known as Queen Anne's Lace in America (and therefore in a lot of the references for wild carrot as a contraceptive and abortifacient). In the UK Queen Anne's Lace is also sometimes the common name for Cow Parsley, *(anthriscus sylveatris)* which is a different plant and does not have the same properties. They are both from the same family and have similar flowers. To gather Wild Carrot seeds yourself you will need to find a good field guide to ensue correct identification as several poisonous look alike occur in the carrot family. However, there is a reliable way to tell it apart from it's lookalikes, and that is the distinctive bristly hairs on it's stem (hence the old saying 'as sure as the hairs on Queen Anne's legs')

Wild carrot seeds have been used for centuries by women all over the world, and their effects have also recently been verified by scientific study. Substances within the seeds have been shown to block progesterone synthesis in pregnant animals. The substance (an antiprogestin) blocks the receptor sites for progesterone in the womb lining, thus depriving the womb of the progesterone that is needed to form a supportive environment to the fertilised egg.

Wild Carrot seeds have a reputation as an effective implantation inhibitor and have been used successfully as an emergency contraceptive. They are also renowned as a natural contraceptive method. In order to successfully use the seeds as a contraceptive, you will need to monitor your menstrual cycles and be able to predict when you will ovulate. Seeds would be taken throughout your fertile period to prevent pregnancy, and although I would not regard this as a fail-safe method I have read reports from women who swear by it.

Dosage

Chew one teaspoon of Wild Carrot seeds per day washed down with water. (you must chew the seeds thoroughly otherwise they will pass through your system without being digested.)
  They can be used in several ways:

- Daily throughout the menstrual cycle.
- The day after unprotected sex - herbal lore is that this would be enough to prevent pregnancy, but modem herbal wisdom states that you should continue for 7-10 days.
- Used throughout your fertile period (if you know your cycle) and for six days following ovulation.

Safety

Women with a history of kidney or gall stones should consult a herbalist before using this herb.

Anyone taking the contraceptive pill, any other oestrogen medication should avoid these herbs, as should anyone who's been advised against taking estrogenic medication (like the contraceptive pill).

Possible side effects

The majority of women report no side effects with this herb, although if constipation occurs, increase the amount of water taken. As Wild Carrot is an oestrogenic herb it can have oestrogen related side effects e.g. abnormal blood clotting, liver problems. and oestrogen dependant tumours.

Further reading on Wild Carrot seeds:

- http://website.lineonc.net/~stolarczyk/queen.hbnl or go to The World Carrot Museum at www.carrotmuseum.com and follow the link for 'Wild'.
- http:f/www.altnature.com/gallery/Wild_Carrot.htm

wild carrot
daucus carota
shoot, flower, leaves and seeds

Tansy

(Tanacetum Vulgare)

Tansy is best known for its insect repellent qualities but has been reported since the eleventh century as having emmenagogual powers. It's a farily toxic plant containing the chemical thujone which causes uterine contractions but is also a brain stimulant. Whilst this herb must be used with caution, it is safe as long as doses are not exceeded.

Susan Weed reports it to be successful at inducing abortion even when menstruation is several weeks late. It is possible (although unconfirmed) that tansy and vitamin C cancel each other out, so they shouldn't be used together.

The amount of thujone present in tansy is highly variable and some plants can contain no traces of it while others produce oil up to 95% thujone. Therefore with every new batch, start out at a low dose in order to test your sensitivity, watching closely for side effects, and increase the dose if necessary.

Dosage

Dosage is contained in one of the recipes given in the blue cohosh section where it is used along with pennyroyal. Tansy can also be used on its own.

Infusion: Steep for 30 minutes. Use ½-1 teaspoon of dried herb per cup, three to four times per day, for up to seven days.

Tincture: ¼-¼ teaspoon in warm water, three to four times a day.

Safety

Anyone prone to epileptic seizures should not use tansy or any other herb containing thujone. Never ingest essential oils - tansy is particularly toxic.

Possible side effects

Nausea, vomiting, inflammation of stomach lining, dilated pupils, weakened or rapid pulse. Tansy has been known to cause temporary lumps in breasts. Tansy can cause women who usually menstruate very heavily to haemorrhage. It is phototoxic, so the user may develop skin rash or blistering in strong sunlight. As with several other herbs in this pamphlet tansy could cause birth defects if the pregnancy were carried to term.

Tansy
Tanacetum Vulgare

Mugwort

(Artemisia Vulgaris)

Mugwort is a well known around the world as a menstrual promoter but not much has been written about its powers as an abortifacient. Like Tansy and juniper, it contains the uterine contractor chemical thujone, and so is fairly toxic.

Dosage

The leaves arc the part of the plant used. Uni Tiamat writes that it's best when used ten days prior to the onset of menstruation and that it's often combined with pennyroyal or ginger.

Infusion: Steep for 15-20 minutes, take 1 teaspoon-1 tablespoon four to six times a day.

Tincture: 30-60 drops (½-1 teaspoon)four to six times a day.

Safety

Nobody prone to epileptic seizures should use this herb or any other herb containing thujone. Thujone is a teratogen and could cause severe birth defects if the pregnancy were carried to term.

Possible side effects

Large prolonged doses (over two weeks) are said to injure the nervous system.

Mugwort
Artemisia Vulgaris
shoots and leaves

Juniper

(Juniperus Communis)

Juniper works as a uterine stimulant and, like mugwort and tansy, it contains thujone so it is fairly toxic. It has a long history as an abortifacient - the stereotypical use of a bottle of gin is derived from the fact of gin being a form of week juniper tincture!

One source claims that juniper.is best used either in the first two weeks of pregnancy or in the first few days after a missed period. Juniper is reputed to work as an implantation inhibitor as well as an abortifacient and has a reputation as a contraceptive.

Dosage

Sometimes combined with Rue. The berries and leaves are used.
  Infustion: (ripe berries) Steep for 10-20 minutes. Take 60-80 mls 2-3 times a day (leaves) steep for 10-20 ins take 1-3 tablespoons 2-3 times a day
  Tincture: (ripe berries)5-20 drops, 2-3 times a day
  Oil: 1-3 drops 2-3 times a day

The root may have implantation-inhibiting properties but I have no reference for appropriate doses.

Fully grown but unripe berries are said to contain higher concentrations of essential oil and so dosages should be reduced if making preparations with them. .

Safety

Anyone with an existing kidney complaint or nerve damage should not use juniper. As juniper contains thujone it should not be used by anyone prone to epileptic seizures.

Possible side effects

Jun r may interfere with the absorption of iron and other essential minerals. May increase the volume of urine and give the urine the odour of violets. Has a tendency to irritate the kidneys (follow up with nettle tea to soothe kidneys after using Juniper).

Juniper
Juniperus Communis
branch and berries

Cotton Root Bark

(Gossypium Hirsutum)

Cotton root bark has a long history as an abortifacient amongst Native American and African women. It is thought to have been used extensively among slave women in cotton plantations in the USA after rape by slave owners.

Cotton root contains gossypol, a substance sold in China for its ability to reduce the male sperm count.

Chinese researchers have found that cotton root bark definitely contains elements with the ability to disrupt pregnancy. It seems to work in two ways. Firstly it acts on the corpus luteum which is a small yellow body foundin the ovary that secretes progesterone to prepare the womb lining for pregnancy. Cotton root disrupts this production of progesterone. The second effect is that it increases receptor sites on oxytocin-sensitive cells, in other words it increases the effect of oxytocin, a hormone which causes uterine contractions.

The main problem with cotton root bark is that it's very hard to obtain. Commercially grown cotton should not be used as it is sprayed with highly toxic chemicals, as the root is not intended for consumption. Use only organically grown cotton.

Dosage

Decoction: 100g of dried cotton root bark to l litre of water. Boil for 20-30 minutes until liquid is reduced to half. Take 2-4 tablespoons every 30-60 minutes.

Tincture: 1-4 teaspoons every 30-60 minutes

Possible side effects

Susan Weed calls it 'the safest and most certain herbal abortifacient'. Although tests have shown prolonged use can be harmful (atrophy of the uterine lining), for the times we're talking about here (no more than 14 days) this shouldn't be a problem.

Parsley

(petroselinum crispum)

Parsley is a mild emmenagogue (a stimulator of menstruation). It works like a charm for starting menstruation when pregnancy is not the cause for delay.

To assist herbal abortion

For terminating a pregnancy, parsley is a helper herb, relaxing the cervix to aid in the release of material from the womb. When used by itself it will not cause abortion. It can be used as a tea or as a pessary and combines well with vitamin C (ascorbic acid).

Parsley Pessary (vaginal insert)

This is a commonly used method. It directly affects the cervix, softening it, helping it to open to prepare for release. Take 2-4 sprigs of parsley, rinse and remove the larger part of the stem just below the first leaf joint After rinsing them, push them inside the vagina as far back as you can, placing them against the cervix. They will feel bulky at first, but they will often soften from your body heat. Change it every twelve hours. To remove the pessary, reach inside with your first two fingers and scoop out the softened herb, look for any blood, then discard. Replace with fresh parsley. You could also tie a string around the stems before insertion to assist in removal.

Making tea from parsley

Whenever available, use the fresh herb. It is readily available in greengrocers and supermarkets. Fill a small to medium sized pan with water and bring to the boil. Remove from the heat and add a handful or two of chopped parsley, cover tightly and let it steep for 20-30 minutes. Strain the tea and compost the herb material. The resulting tea is green in colour. If you don't like the taste you can sweeten it and/or add milk.

Safety

Parsley is not toxic, but it should not be used by people with inflammatory kidney problems or other kidney conditions.

There are no reported side effects.

Parsley
petroselinum crispum

Black Cohosh

(Cimicifuga racemosa)

This is an anti-spasmodic herb often used in conjunction with blue cohosh. Black cohosh is unlikely to cause abortion unless combined with other herbs. It is a helper herb, helping to prepare the cervix to release the contents of the uterus. It is often combined with blue cohosh, and it also combines well with vitamin C and dong quai.

Black cohosh is valuable for treating PMT, menstrual cramps, hormonal imbalances and menopause symptoms. It also has a balancing effect on hormone production, particularly oestrogen.

Dosage

The root is the part used.

Decoction: simmer 1-4 tablespoons for 5-15 minutes, 3-4 times a day.

Tincture: ¼-1 teaspoon, 3-4 times a day.

Capsules: Dosages can be in the range of 500mg-1,000mg every four hours.

*Infustion:*Steep 2 teaspoons in 500ml of water. Take 2-3 tablespoons 6 times a day.

Safety

Black cohosh can depress heart rate. Anyone with any type of heart disease should not use this herb. Due to its oestrogenic properties, this herb should not be taken by anyone who has been advised no to take the Pill. Black. cohosh should not be combined with anti-depressants.

Possible side effects

Dizziness, diarrhoea, nausea, headaches, shakes, low pulse, vomiting. Side effects possible with prolonged use may include uterine irritation, abdominal pain. abnormal blood clotting (which could cause problems when using herbs to end pregnancy, such as possible haemorrhage), liver problems.Because of its oestrogenic properties, it may also encourage oestrogen-dependent tumours.

However, in five different studies using doses equivalent to 40 mg/day of crude herb there were no case reports of toxic effects from the herb,and there appears to be no specific toxicity associated with any of its known constituents. A few side effects were noted; dizziness, headache and weight gain.

Ginger Root

Ginger Root
Zinzibar Officinalis

(Zinzibar Officinalis)

This is a helper herb, not potent enough to cause abortion in its own. Its readily available as a foodstuff and extremely effective at bringing on menstruation when not pregnant. Susan Weed calls it 'one of the strongest and fastest acting emmenagogues'.

Ginger is believed to be very good at enhancing the effectiveness of any other herbs with which it is combined.

Dosage

The root is used.

Decoction: Simmer for 15-30 minutes.Take 2-4 tablespoons, 4-6 times a day.

Tincture: 1-4 drops, 4-6 times a day.

Possible side effects

Can be nauseating in large doses.

Ginger Root
Zinzibar Officinalis

Chapter 26

Bibliography

Hoffman, David. 1996. 'The Holistic Herbal, A Safe and Practical Guide to Making and Using Herbal Remedies' Element Books (an imprint of Harper Collins). ISBN 0-00-713301-4

Chalker, Rebecca & Downer. Carol. 1992. 'A Woman's book of choices - Abortion, Menstrual Extraction, RU486' Four Walls Eight Windows. ISBN 0-941423-86-7

Culpepper, Nicholas. First published 1649, 1963 edition edited by David Potterton. 'Culpepper's Colour Herbal' W. Foulsham & Co. Ltd. ISBN 0-572-01153-0

Riddle, John M. 1997. 'Eve's Herbs - A History of Contraception and Abortion In the West' Harvard University Press. ISBN 0-874-27026-6

Tiamat, Uni M. 1994. 'Herbal Abortion • The fruit of the Tree of Knowledge' Sage-Femme. ISBN 0-964520-3-7 (available from Sage-Femme 3457 N. University, Suite 120, Peoria, IL 61604-1322, USA)

Weed, Susan S. 1996.'Wise Woman Herbal For the Childbearing Year' Ash Tree Publishing. ISBN 0-9614620-0—0 Although this book is mainly about herbs for pregnancy and childbirth it has a chapter at the beginning about herbs to terminate pregnancy

The following book is quoted in this pamphlet but I've not actually been able to find a copy of it. Anything I've got from it has been through other sources.

Gardner, Joy 1985. 'Abortion -A Personal Approach' Heal Yourself Press, Seattle, Washington, USA

Websites

Sister Zeus 'Fertility Awareness, Herbs affecting the Menstrual Cycle, Herbal Contraception & Herbal Abortion' This is a very comprehensive website containing huge amounts of useful information. There is no other website like it. The section where women give their personal accounts of herbal abortion (called 'Sharing our wisdom') is an invaluable read www.sister_zeus.com

Herbal Fertility Control: Contraception and Abortion www.orgonelab. org/contracep.htm

Email Support Group

This Is for women going through herbal abortion and women who want to support these women. This is an invaluable group providing support on a practical and emotional level. There are several women very experienced in guiding people through herbal abortion and many who've recently been through It themselves. I strongly recommend joining this group, as you will then have women on hand to answer any questions or concerns you may have.

http://groups.yahoo.com/grouplherbal_abortion_support

Chapter 27

Abortlfacient - Any substance that has the ability to terminate pregnancy. A term used to describe any strong Emmenagogue.

Antispasmodic - Relieves, or prevents spasms.Relaxes smooth muscles like the uterus and the intestines.

Cervix - neck of the uterus located at the top of the vagina (**cervical** - of, or relating to, the cervix)

Chorionic Villi - Root-like structures of the fertilised eggs cell membrane, which attach to the uterus and form the placenta.

Corpus huteum - A yellow body which develops in the ovary after the release of the egg. It only remains existence if pregnancy has begun.

Decoction - A water-based herbal preparation where the water and herb are simmered on the heat together in a pan. The recipe for a standard decoction id given on page 25.

Ectopic Pregnancy - When the fertilised egg begins to develop outside the womb (e.g. in the fallopian tube) which can be very serious as the growing egg could rupture the fallopian tube.

Embryo - Human offspring in the first eight weeks from conception

Emmenagogue - Any substance that induces or hastens menstruation. In this pamphlet it's taken to mean a substance that is not strong enough to cause abortion by itself but could induce menstruation if pregnancy is not the cause (i.e. weak emmenagogues). There is overlap with the term abortincient as all abortifacients are emmenagogues, but not all emmenagogues are abortifacients.

Fallopian tube - Either of the two muscular hollow arms of the uterus that guide the egg tot he uterus. Fertilisation usually occurs in the fallopian tubes.

Foetus - A human offspring more than eight weeks since conception.

Haemorrhage - Profuse bleeding.

Infusion - A water-based herbal preparation where the water is boiled first and then poured over the herb. The recipe for a standard infusion is given on page 25.

Oestrogen - A female hormone.

Os - The muscular opening to the uterus

Ovary - One of the pair of female reproductive glands that produces eggs

Ovulation - The releasing of eggs from the ovary. This happens on a cyclical basis as part of the woman's menstrual cycle.

Oxytocin - A hormone that induces contractions of the uterus.

Placenta - All organ which connects the foetus to the uterus, passing nourishment to it through the umbilical cord.

Progesterone - A hormone produced by the corpus luteum causing the uterine wall to become thicken and act as a fertile bed for the egg.

Steep - To soak in liquid

Teratogen - A substance that causes malformation of an embryo.

Tincture - A herbal preparation where the active ingredients of a plant are extracted in alcohol. The recipe for a standard tincture is given on page 26.

Uterus - the womb (**uterine**- of, or relating to, the womb)

Made in the USA
Monee, IL
23 December 2024

75220890R00046